ALKALINE SMOOTHIES

LEGAL NOTICE

Copyright (c) 2018 Seb Infante.

All rights are reserved. No portion of this book may be reproduced or duplicated using any form whether mechanical, electronic, or otherwise. No portion of this book may be transmitted, stored in a retrieval database, or otherwise made available in any manner whether public or private unless specific permission is granted by the publisher. Vector illustration credit: vecteezy.com

This book does not offer advice, but merely provides information. The author offers no advice whether medical, financial, legal, or otherwise, nor does the author encourage any person to pursue any specific course of action discussed in this book. This book is not a substitute for professional advice. The reader accepts complete and sole responsibility for the manner in which this book and its contents are used. The publisher and the author will not be held liable for any damages caused.

*"Let food be thy medicine
and medicine be thy food."*

Hippocrates

Rebalance Your pH

Restore Your Vitality

Alkaline Smoothies

*Top 50 Alkaline Diet Approved Smoothies and Drinks
to Detox, Rebalance Your pH, and Feel Decades Younger*

Seb Infante

6 – Alkaline Smoothies

Contents

How I Rebalanced My Life	10
Introduction to Alkaline Smoothies	12
Watermelon Strawberry Smoothie	27
Watermelon Kale Smoothie	28
Mix Berry Watermelon Smoothie	29
Healthy Green Smoothie	30
Apple Spinach Cucumber Smoothie	31
Refreshing Lime Smoothie	32
Broccoli Green Smoothie	33
Healthy Vegetable Smoothie	34
Refreshing Green Smoothie	35
Sweet Green Smoothie	36
Avocado Mango Smoothie	37
Super Healthy Green Smoothie	38
Spinach Kale Green Smoothie	39
Spinach Coconut Almond Smoothie	40
Pear Kale Smoothie	41
Banana Peach Smoothie	42
Refreshing Alkaline Smoothie	43
Almond Carrot Smoothie	44
Blueberry Almond Smoothie	45

Kiwi Cucumber Boosting Smoothie	46
Spinach Protein Smoothie	47
Tropical Smoothie	48
Berry Kale Smoothie	49
Basil Kale Strawberry Smoothie	50
Chia Strawberry Smoothie	51
Strawberry Banana Smoothie	52
Spinach Berry Smoothie	53
Graprefruit Spinach Smoothie	54
Coconut Smoothie	55
Pear Spinach Smoothie	56
Detox Avocado Smoothie	57
Almond Blueberry Smoothie	58
Avocado Blueberry Smoothie	59
Vegan Blueberry Smoothie	60
Berry Peach Smoothie	61
Kiwi Green Smoothie	62
Lemon Pineapple Smoothie	63
Raspberry Chia Smoothie	64
Orange Mango Avocado Smoothie	65
Green Detox Smoothie	66
Apricot Spinach Smoothie	67
Healthy Melon Smoothie	68
Cantaloupe Lemon Smoothie	69

8 – Alkaline Smoothies

Frosty Watermelon Smoothie	70
Apple Beet Smoothie	71
Matcha Green Smoothie	72
Alkaline Super Smoothie	73
Tomato Avocado Smoothie	74
Spinach Peach Banana Smoothie	75
Salty Green Smoothie	76
The "Dirty Dozen" And "Clean 15"	77
Measurement Conversion Tables	78
Alphabetical Recipe Index	79

How I Rebalanced My Life

Up until about a year ago, I had a lot of trouble with my weight, my overall health, and I also had a serious problem with developing a healthy relationship with my body. It took me a very long time to get used to the idea that something would have to change, because I had developed so many unhealthy habits over the years that I honestly thought I would never be able to get rid of them and live a normal life. I did a lot of research online, and after reading into more detail about the Alkaline Diet, I realized that it described precisely the things that were wrong with the way I was eating.

So many people today have simply never had a healthy relationship with food, and I have to admit that this is something I used to be guilty of as well. When I was younger, my meals were full of processed food, meat, refined sugar, and a lot of fizzy drinks. The sad part is that I didn't realize just how much that food was affecting me in a negative way. Until I discovered the Alkaline Diet, I never even knew that these foods were causing a serious acid issue inside my body. It now made sense why I was always feeling so bad about myself, and why it was always so difficult for me to lose any weight.

The 50 Alkaline Smoothies that you will find in the pages of this book, quite literally, completely changed the way that I live my life! They are very easy to make, the ingredients are super affordable, and there are also so many recipe varieties of these smoothies that literally everyone's taste can be accounted for! No matter which part of the world you live in, you can use the organic, seasonal ingredients in your area of the world to create these delicious smoothies, and even to experiment a little bit with your own recipe ideas!

Ever since I started this diet years ago, I have been able to fix my weight issues and also to finally fix my blood test results, so that now all of the numbers in my blood test are in the correct areas, without any danger of me developing any illnesses. These smoothies were so convenient for me because they were easy to prepare and plan, and they were also incredibly convenient to take with me on the go! My meals at work were one of the main reasons why I had gained so much weight, because I was eating and drinking things that just weren't very good for me. However, the smoothies ensured that I felt full and that I wouldn't eat any of the fast food and other junk that tasted good, but was so bad for me. I even managed to include my family into the mix, and I proceeded to make smoothies for them as well! Everyone was delighted with the results. My entire family is feeling better and stronger, and also losing weight. These 50 alkaline smoothies have become a very important part of my life, and I hope that you too will also be able to discover their benefits, so that you may live a longer and healthier life too!

Yours in good health and vitality,
Seb Infante

Introduction to Alkaline Smoothies

Before we move on to talking about the actual smoothies and why they are so important for this diet in the form of a smoothie, we must first understand what the Alkaline Diet actually is and why the smoothies are so important when it comes to making the diet actually work for you.

There are so many different diets on the market, and they all claim that they can help you reach the magic number on a scale. However, because each one of us is different, so are the diets that help us to get to our goal weight. But when it comes to the Alkaline Diet, there are additionally so many health benefits that will come with this diet, which are the things that truly make the diet worth it.

WHAT IS THE ALKALINE DIET?

The Alkaline Diet is based on the theory that certain foods are the culprits when it comes to making our bodies produce higher levels of acid. All bodies have a certain level of acid within them, however, if these levels suddenly go up above average, they can cause serious health issues and a very groggy feeling about your life overall.

Do you ever feel like you just can't focus on what you are doing, or you often feel depressed? Food is often the cause for these problems, and when this is the case, you need to make sure that you check your diet first before you move on to looking for any other causes for your problems.

The Alkaline Diet starts by informing you that the foods that are causing you the most problems are refined sugar, all processed foods, meta, wheat, and a few other foods which we will discuss below. The great thing about these restrictions is that these are the foods that you should not be eating anyway. Processed food, for example, brings absolutely no benefits for your body, which is why it is such a good idea to get rid of it as soon as possible. These are the kinds of foods that will really cause the level of acid to increase in your system, which is when all of the bad side effects will suddenly become present as well.

Food that Are Good and Bad for You on this Diet

Since you know that there will be many delicious smoothies for you in the future of this diet, you need to first understand what it is that you can and cannot add to your smoothies in terms of food. Please remember though, that you really need to stick to the right foods and not mess with the ingredients. Even though you may sometimes feel that you miss certain foods a lot, and you really have a need to add them to your smoothies, please don't do this. If you add foods that are bad for you and that will be increasing your acid levels, then you will ruin all of the hard work that you have been doing up until now. Even one mistake is enough to set you back a few days, so instead of giving up, be determined and stick to this diet until you reach the weight and health level that you are happy with.

Foods that are good for you

The best foods for you to choose on this diet are almost all fruits and vegetables, legumes, tofu, nuts, and seeds. These are, luckily, very affordable ingredients that many people can find in their local sore, which is why this diet is so easy to maintain. These delicious ingredients are also the reason why the smoothies are so great and why they can be adapted to fit any meal of the day.

Foods that are not good for you

Technically, everything that isn't on the list of foods that are good for you is automatically bad for you. Some examples of foods that you really shouldn't eat are eggs, meat, dairy, grains, all processed food, canned food, and anything else that isn't wholefoods should be avoided. This also includes alcohol and coffee. If you're worried about low energy levels because you will not be able to have coffee, don't worry! Tea is actually a much better way to bring your energy levels up, and it also won't mess with the acid levels within your system.

What do you need to get started on this diet?

When people decide that they are about to commit to a new diet, it isn't surprising that people were feeling stressed and weren't sure if they would ever be able to complete the diet properly. If you are one of these people, don't feel so bad about yourself! You are only human after all, and it is perfectly normal that you have days when you absolutely do not feel like doing anything, and certainly when you don't feel like going through with a diet. However, the great thing about the Alkaline Diet is that it is so easy to implement it into your daily life and also find all of the ingredients that are so necessary in order to make sure that you complete this diet successfully and to then be able to add elements of this diet throughout your life.

One thing that will be difficult at the start

We must be realistic when it comes to switching you to a new kind of diet. One of the biggest problems that people face is the ability to let go of the foods that they were so used to eating for years. This is especially true for refined sugar and also foods that are super high in carbohydrates. Sugar is an incredibly addictive ingredient. It takes some people months before they are fully able to completely let go of sugar in their lives. You make this easier for yourself by creating a fun calendar for your diet and marking off every day that you have successfully completed without eating the foods that are bad for you. This will be a great way to motivate yourself, and you will also be able to look back proudly on how much you have achieved and far you've come since starting the alkaline smoothies.

How to plan your shopping

One of the great things about this diet is that you can easily plan your future grocery shopping and your budget! Because the smoothies have specific recipes and measurements for each one, you can easily purchase groceries for the whole week, and maybe even for the whole month! This is very important because grocery shopping one thing that makes people really annoyed with diets. If you enter a supermarket without any set plan, you will be most likely to just buy whatever is quick and convenient o eat, which will completely ruin the purpose and the hard work that you've put into your diet. Do not do this to your health. Instead, just take a few minutes to plan the ingredients according to your own budget, and you will soon be on your way to weight loss and overall health!

You don't need anyone else's help

Some diets require a lot of research and also support from other people in order to be completed properly. This just adds an extra level of time and worry for people, especially those who have many failed diet attempts behind them.

Unlike these diets, the Alkaline Diet does not require you to seek help from anyone else. As long as you understand which foods are good for you and which ones are not, and as long as you are consistent with your smoothies, then that is all you need to be successful in this diet. This is such a great relief for people who have a difficult time for diets overall, because imagine having one more thing to worry about when you are already trying to change your way of eating for the better?

Do you need exercise?

Please read this section carefully, because exercise is often a completely misunderstood concept when it comes to dieting and a healthy lifestyle. No, for the Alkaline Diet itself, you do not need any exercise. This is because the diet focuses entirely on the correct working of your digestive system, so as long as it is working properly, your health will be working properly too.

However, this does not mean that exercise should not be done at all. It is understandable that people are busy and not huge fans of exercise in general, however, you really do need to move around, not because of the diet, but because of your overall health.

Most of us have horrible sedentary jobs, which are worsening our health on a daily basis even without us truly realizing that this is happening. There is nothing worse than spending hours sitting in the same spot. You cut off blood circulation, not only to your heart and lungs, but also to the many tiny capillaries inside your body. When these capillaries do not receive any oxygen for a long time, they will eventually die out, which is truly a horrible thing for your body to happen!

Also, when you spend a long time just sitting, you are causing almost every single muscle in your body to drastically weaken. This also includes the muscles in your spine, which then are not strong enough to help you sit upright. This ruins your posture almost entirely, and can cause you horrible health problems in the future.

So, even though you don't specifically need exercise for this diet, you do need exercise in your overall life. If you are really not the kind of person who likes to be active, then choose something that you enjoy. Even something as simple as long, daily walk can really help to boost your overall health and make you a happier person.

Do you need to buy any extra products for this diet?

Absolutely not. You do not need to buy anything other than the wholefoods that you will need for creating the delicious alkaline smoothies. You will often see in supermarkets that almost every diet in the world has 'instant' products ready to be purchased on the shelves to seemingly make this easier for you. However, this is far from the truth.

Even if the product in the supermarket is labelled as being specifically for the diet that you are on, it is still a product that has been processed. And remember what we said about processed foods earlier on and how bad they are for you? Do not ruin the work that you put into your body by purchasing something that is about to make the situation even worse. Instead, remember that smoothies are something that you can easily take with you no matter where you are going. Simply choose your favourite smoothie recipe, and make it to the size that is easy to carry around with you. Even a habit as simple as this one can mean the difference between a successful diet and a failed one. You can do it!

How Does the Alkaline Diet Work?

In order to understand why alkaline foods are so important, you need to first understand what it is that they do to our bodies and why they are so helpful.

If you remember your science class way back in school, you will remember the measurement called the pH (power of Hydrogen) factor. It measures how acidic or alkaline something is. It is used in all areas of life, including your body of course. The scale goes from 0 to 14. O means that something is entirely acidic. 14 means that something is entirely alkaline. The number 7 defined a neutral state of pH levels.

Not every area of your body has the same pH levels by the way. It depend which organ we are referring to, which part of the body we are looking at, and what the purpose of that particular part of the body is. For example, your blood is somewhat alkaline, which a measurement that usually ranges around 7.45. this of course makes sense because you wouldn't want something that is acidic to be going through your blood stream. Likewise, your stomach is very acidic, with a pH scale of about 3.5 or even less! Again, this makes perfect sense because you use the acid in your stomach to digest food, and also to destroy harmful things that you may have accidentally ingested.

So on which part of the scale is the Alkaline Diet aiming at?

Well, because your blood is so important for the correct function of your entire body, the ideal level that needs to be maintained in the majority of your body is the slightly alkaline levels of 7.45. Whether or not your body reaches these levels depends on a number of different things, such as illnesses, lifestyle, and even genetics, but one of the best ways to maintain the proper levels is through the right foods!

This is why it is so important to always be weary of the foods that you are eating and in which amounts. When you eat something that is bad for your body, it won't just disappear. Your body will need to deal with it, digest it, and decide which parts of it need to be completely eliminated. And in cases where your body is not able to handle this situation on its own, you will end up with an illness, because the bad things that you were eating for such a long time will cause enough acid and toxins to overtake your body. Why would you want that for your system?

The best way for you and your body to work as a team, is to make sure that you are only eating the foods which make both your body and your mind feel great, so that you can have a happy and productive life.

Health Benefits of the Alkaline Diet and Its Smoothies

Now that you know why the Alkaline Diet is so good for you, and what exactly it does to change the internal system of your body, it makes perfect sense that there must be many things that this diet is going to help you with when it comes to your overall health, as well as any present or future illnesses.

There is plenty of scientific evidence that supports the fact that foods that are high in acid levels (such as protein and cheese) are often a cause of aggravated **kidney stones**. The acidic level in these foods makes it difficult for your body to clear out toxins properly through your urine, which means that some of the toxins will remain in your kidneys, causing trouble.

Next, the fact that you will be able to keep your blood alkaline levels stable also means that it will help to keep your veins, arteries, and capillaries healthy for a long time! This will ensure the **health of your heart** because your heart will have enough oxygen to work with as it pumps blood throughout your system.

Strong levels of oxygen within your body will also ensure that your muscles and your bones will stay healthy and strong, which is especially important if you are looking to have a healthy and active life even in your older age. It will also reduce back pain, and the risk of diabetes.

The food that we eat has such a huge impact on how our bodies behave and how much energy we have. For example, if you don't take care of the food that you are consuming, you will also make it much more difficult for your brain to have the right amount of oxygen and nutrients to function. This is often **the cause of depression**, and in some cases, it confuses people into thinking that they have clinical depression, when in fact they are just eating a very poor choice of foods, which is not allowing the brain or the mind to function properly. You need a very complex set of nutrients and minerals for all of the cognitive functions in your brain, so you need to make sure that you are truly taking care of this vital organ.

How Do the Smoothies Help Weight Loss?

You may be thinking, all of this health stuff is great, but how will these smoothies also help me to lose weight?

People often think is this complex process that requires you to follow an extremely specific diet and exercise ritual before you actually see any results. However, this is not true. Your body does a number of things in automatic mode, it is only the cognitive side of your mind that allows you to distinguish between these terms of exercise and diet. The rest of your body, and your organs in particular, don't have such comprehension, they only know what they are programmed to do. If you eat bad food, your organs have to deal with toxins and excess at which has not been burned off (thus is stored in your bum). If you eat good food, your body has what it needs to run smoothly, and it won't face any bumps in the road.

Therefore, when it comes to weight loss, the alkaline smoothies are a wonderful addition to your life because they will provide your body with everything it needs to run, and it also won't bother you with endless formulas on what the best way to lose weight might actually be. Wouldn't it be great to be able to reduce all of this stress and simply get used to living a life where you are always eating well and helping your body? This is all you need to lose weight with the alkaline smoothies. Your body will set itself up for its own routine, and in turn, will help you to shed any weight that you should not be carrying.

What's also great is that the weight loss effect doesn't take a long time to start at all. After just a few days of eating right and helping your system recover from toxins and any problems that it might have had to deal with, you will notice positive changes and a much healthier way to live life. Make the right decision now, and start a life that will benefit you long into the future.

The Best Foods for Alkaline Smoothies and How They Help

Now that you have a good understanding of the Alkaline Diet and why it is of so much help for you, let's look at some of the best ingredients that you should put in your smoothies and how they help your system. You can either follow a recipe precisely, or you can later make your own combinations of alkaline smoothies once you get used to them. Either way, the best way to make the most out of these smoothies is to know exactly which foods are the right ones to use and what exactly they do to help your body feel great!

Anything that's super green!

Any food that is really green, especially dark green, is great for your alkaline smoothie. But only if it is organic and not processed of course! We are specifically referring to spinach, kale, broccoli, dandelion greens, radish greens, etc. These foods are super high in antioxidants and they will provide your body with an incredible amount of energy! You can choose whichever foods are native to your area of the world, because this will make it both a lot easier to buy them, and it will also be cheaper. Do keep in mind one thing do. Although these greens are very healthy for you, it is important to rotate them around a little so that your body doesn't get used to them. Switch between kale and spinach for example every few days, and then think of another recipe that would go even better with these ingredients. The more you play around with your smoothies and your greens, to more your body will get out of this entire situation!

Probiotic Powder

Although we do not encourage other additives to be used in your alkaline smoothies, probiotic powder can be found in organic forms, and is especially good for people who are only just now starting a diet. The powder will help to provide your stomach with friendly bacteria, which will help to digest food and to make you feel better both before and after meals. You don't need to use a lot of this product at all! Half of a spoonful will be enough to give you all the benefits that your body needs from healthy, organic probiotics.

Celtic Sea Salt

Salt in large quantities is certainly not good for you, and this is especially true for the general, unhealthy salt that we often find in our kitchens, and that many restaurants use to prepare our food. However, salt is part of our bodies, which means that we do need small amounts of it in order to help us reach a more alkaline state. Celtic Sea Salt is especially great for this purpose because it is full of minerals that really help to boost your system, and that help your body find toxins and illnesses that it really doesn't need. Use only a small pinch of salt in your smoothies, and only once a day. This will be enough for your body to get all the salt it needs for the day.

Berries

Any kind of berries are a great addition to your smoothie. Not only will they help to add an additional layer of taste because they have a bit of sugar in them, but also because they are super high in antioxidants which will help you feel better and will also increase the process of weight loss. As with any other food, make sure that you also switch your berries around so that you don't become bored with a single flavour. Make sure to choose the berries that are easily produced in your own part of the world, so that you are not getting frozen products from the other side of the world. Gentle fruits like berries easily lose much of their vitamins and minerals during transport, so getting ingredients that are organic from your area helps you to ingest more vitamins and minerals.

Bananas

 No surprise that bananas are here on our list! They have a high level of potassium in them, which is great for your brain and also for your muscles. Bananas are also a great food to coat your stomach, which make digesting other meals that much easier. You can add bananas to any smoothie to add a layer of sweetness and also to improve the texture. Bananas that have been blended up with ice make for a fantastic milkshake, and one that is full of organic ingredients and is actually good for you!

Greek Yoghurt

Yoghurt is excellent for helping your stomach produce good bacteria and also for helping to coat your stomach during digestion. It is a very neutral ingredient and super gentle on both your stomach and your intestines, which means that it is great at helping to soothe your body in case of any infections of toxins that may have passed through. This is a much better way to soothe your system than using medicine would be (unless the medicine is absolutely required). However, make sure that you are only choosing yoghurt that is free of any added sugar or fruit. You don't want to choose any yoghurt that doesn't have organic ingredients inside it because otherwise you will not see any health benefits from it. Yoghurt is also great for giving your alkaline smoothie a better texture.

Coconut Milk

Coconut milk is made from the alkaline flesh of a coconut and coconut water. This is a great ingredient for helping to balance your body's alkaline levels, because it has a good amount of B vitamins and fiber, which are essential for your body and your energy levels. Coconut milk can be sweet, but it often doesn't have a very strong flavour, which means that it was made from organic products. Don't choose coconut milk with added sugar, because you will be causing the opposite effect of actually giving your body the sugar that produces acid. This is not what you want in your alkaline smoothie at all!

Almond Milk

This is also a great addition to your smoothie and will really help to enhance the flavour of your drink. This is a very alkaline product, and it is only beneficial if you are not purchasing almond milk that has added sugar in it. Stay away from all sugar as much as possible. The almond milk itself has plenty of delicious flavours that will help to make your smoothies even better!

When should you drink alkaline smoothies?

There isn't a set time when you should or should not make yourself an alkaline smoothie. They are an incredibly versatile drink, which you can easily blend with both your lifestyle and your budget. You can choose your own ingredients, make them for friends, or make them in advance and store them for up to 48 hours. This is such a great way to make your body feel better and stronger, that the smoothies will easily be adapted to whatever your current lifestyle may be.

There is one thing that you do need to keep in mind though, and that is the amount of calories and sugars that you are adding to your body on a daily basis. This is especially true if you are using the alkaline smoothies to lose weight. Remember that even though you are eating healthy, the same chemical principles still apply. If you are eating too much food an your are not burning up the calories, you will sill end up gaining weight even though the weight might be coming from healthy food. For example, bananas are quite high in calories, so if you are eating too many bananas in a single day, you will still end up gaining weight.

Likewise, you also need to take care about the amount of sugar that you are adding to your system. Although you are welcome to use fruits in your alkaline smoothies, and even though they are super good for you, fruits still contain sugar. Even though it is not the refined sugar that is entirely bad for you, even if you are eating too much of the unrefined sugars, you can still end up gaining weight and causing an increase in acid levels inside your stomach.

Everything you do in life needs to be done in moderation, and alkaline smoothies are no different. If you really love them and want to have them twice a day, a good rule of thumb is to have one super green smoothie (which is high in vitamins and minerals but low in calories) and one fruit smoothie (which will satisfy sugar cravings and is a little higher in calories).

Watermelon Strawberry Smoothie

Serves: 2 / Preparation time: 5 minutes / Cooking time: 5 minutes

1 cup coconut milk yogurt

½ cup strawberries

2 cups fresh watermelon

1 banana

- Add all ingredients to the blender and blend until smooth.
- Serve and enjoy.

Per Serving: Calories 160; Fat 4.5 g; Carbohydrates 33.7 g; Sugar 19.3 g; Protein 1.8 g; Cholesterol 0 mg;

Watermelon Kale Smoothie

Serves: 2 / Preparation time: 5 minutes / Cooking time: 5 minutes

8 oz water

1 orange, peeled

3 cups kale, chopped

1 banana, peeled

2 cups watermelon, chopped

1 carrot, chopped

- Add all ingredients to the blender and blend until smooth and creamy.
- Serve immediately and enjoy.

Per Serving: Calories 203; Fat 0.5 g; Carbohydrates 49.2 g; Sugar 26.7 g; Protein 5.6 g; Cholesterol 0 mg

Mix Berry Watermelon Smoothie

Serves: 2 / Preparation time: 5 minutes / Cooking time: 5 minutes

1 cup evamor

2 fresh lemon juices

¼ cup fresh mint leaves

1 ½ cups mixed berries

2 cups watermelon

- Add all ingredients to the blender and blend until smooth.
- Serve immediately and enjoy.

Per Serving: Calories 122; Fat 1 g; Carbohydrates 26.1 g; Sugar 17.8 g; Protein 2.4 g; Cholesterol 0 mg

Healthy Green Smoothie

Serves: 3 / Preparation time: 5 minutes / Cooking time: 5 minutes

1 cup water

1 fresh lemon, peeled

1 avocado

1 cucumber, peeled

1 cup spinach

1 cup ice cubes

- Add all ingredients to the blender and blend until smooth and creamy.
- Serve immediately and enjoy.

Per Serving: Calories 160; Fat 13.3 g; Carbohydrates 11.6 g; Sugar 2.5 g; Protein 2.4 g; Cholesterol 0 mg

Apple Spinach Cucumber Smoothie

Serves: 1 / Preparation time: 5 minutes / Cooking time: 5 minutes

¾ cup water

½ green apple, diced

¾ cup spinach

½ cucumber

- Add all ingredients to the blender and blend until smooth and creamy.
- Serve immediately and enjoy.

Per Serving: Calories 86; Fat 0.5 g; Carbohydrates 21.7 g; Sugar 14.2 g; Protein 1.9 g; Cholesterol 0 mg

Refreshing Lime Smoothie

Serves: 2 / Preparation time: 5 minutes / Cooking time: 5 minutes

1 cup ice cubes

20 drops liquid stevia

2 fresh lime, peeled and halved

1 tsp lime zest, grated

½ cucumber, chopped

1 avocado, pitted and peeled

2 cups spinach

1 tbsp creamed coconut

¾ cup coconut water

- Add all ingredients to the blender and blend until smooth and creamy.
- Serve immediately and enjoy.

Per Serving: Calories 313; Fat 25.1 g; Carbohydrates 24.7 g; Sugar 5.4 g; Protein 4.9 g; Cholesterol 0 mg

Broccoli Green Smoothie

Serves: 4 / Preparation time: 5 minutes / Cooking time: 5 minutes

1 carrot, peeled and chopped

1 lemon, peeled

1 apple, diced

1 banana

1 cup spinach

½ cup broccoli

- Add all ingredients to the blender and blend until smooth and creamy.
- Serve immediately and enjoy.

Per Serving: Calories 71; Fat 0.3 g; Carbohydrates 18.3 g; Sugar 10.7 g; Protein 1.3 g; Cholesterol 0 mg

Healthy Vegetable Smoothie

Serves: 2 / Preparation time: 5 minutes / Cooking time: 5 minutes

1 cup ice cubes

2 cups fresh spinach

2 celery stalks

½ cup fresh parsley

1 cucumber

1 lemon juice

1 avocado

- Add all ingredients to the blender and blend until smooth and creamy.
- Serve immediately and enjoy.

Per Serving: Calories 248; Fat 20.2 g; Carbohydrates 17.1 g; Sugar 4 g; Protein 4.5 g; Cholesterol 0 mg

Refreshing Green Smoothie

Serves: 2 / Preparation time: 5 minutes / Cooking time: 5 minutes

1 cup ice cubes

½ lemon juice

½ cucumber, chopped

¼ cup parsley

1 cup spinach

½ cup water

¼ cup peaches, sliced

1 banana

- Add all ingredients to the blender and blend until smooth and creamy.
- Serve immediately and enjoy.

Per Serving: Calories 80; Fat 0.5 g; Carbohydrates 19.2 g; Sugar 10.6 g; Protein 2.1 g; Cholesterol 0 mg

Sweet Green Smoothie

Serves: 1 / Preparation time: 5 minutes / Cooking time: 5 minutes

2 tbsp flax seeds

½ cup wheatgrass

1 mango

1 cup pomegranate juice

- Add all ingredients to the blender and blend until smooth and creamy.
- Serve immediately and enjoy.

Per Serving: Calories 376; Fat 5.7 g; Carbohydrates 78.3 g; Sugar 69.1 g; Protein 5.4 g; Cholesterol 0 mg

Avocado Mango Smoothie

Serves: 1 / Preparation time: 5 minutes / Cooking time: 5 minutes

1 cup ice cubes

½ cup mango

½ avocado

1 tbsp ginger

3 kale leaves

1 cup coconut water

- Add all ingredients to the blender and blend until smooth.
- Serve and enjoy.

Per Serving: Calories 269; Fat 3.6 g; Carbohydrates 53.2 g; Sugar 17.7 g; Protein 11 g; Cholesterol 0 mg;

Super Healthy Green Smoothie

Serves: 2 / Preparation time: 5 minutes / Cooking time: 5 minutes

1 tsp spirulina powder

1 cup coconut water

2 cups mixed greens

1 tbsp ginger

4 tbsp lemon juice

2 celery stalks

1 cup cucumber, chopped

1 green pear, core removed

1 banana

- Add all ingredients to the blender and blend until smooth and creamy.
- Serve immediately and enjoy.

Per Serving: Calories 161; Fat 1.1 g; Carbohydrates 37.3 g; Sugar 20.3 g; Protein 3.9 g; Cholesterol 0 mg

Spinach Kale Green Smoothie

Serves: 2 / Preparation time: 5 minutes / Cooking time: 5 minutes

16 oz water

1 tbsp ground flax seed

½ tbsp parsley, minced

1 tbsp lemon juice

1 celery stalk

½ green apple

½ cucumber

1 cup kale

1 cup spinach

- Add all ingredients to the blender and blend until smooth and creamy.
- Serve immediately and enjoy.

Per Serving: Calories 82; Fat 1.4 g; Carbohydrates 15.9 g; Sugar 7.5 g; Protein 2.9 g; Cholesterol 0 mg

Spinach Coconut Almond Smoothie

Serves: 2 / Preparation time: 5 minutes / Cooking time: 5 minutes

2 tbsp unsweetened coconut flakes

3 cups fresh pineapple

½ cup coconut water

1½ cups almond milk

2 cups fresh spinach

- Add all ingredients to the blender and blend until smooth and creamy.
- Serve immediately and enjoy.

Per Serving: Calories 204; Fat 3.9 g; Carbohydrates 42.8 g; Sugar 30.6 g; Protein 3.6 g; Cholesterol 0 mg

Pear Kale Smoothie

Serves: 2 / Preparation time: 5 minutes / Cooking time: 5 minutes

1 cup apple juice

1 cup water

¼ cup mint leaves

2 cups kale

1 ripe pear, cored and chopped

- Add all ingredients to the blender and blend until smooth and creamy.
- Serve immediately and enjoy.

Per Serving: Calories 135; Fat 0.3 g; Carbohydrates 32.5 g; Sugar 18.8 g; Protein 2.7 g; Cholesterol 0 mg

Banana Peach Smoothie

Serves: 2 / Preparation time: 5 minutes / Cooking time: 5 minutes

1 cup coconut water

1 tsp agave syrup

1¼ oz spinach

1 banana

1 ripe peach

- Add all ingredients to the blender and blend until smooth and creamy.
- Serve immediately and enjoy.

Per Serving: Calories 120; Fat 0.7 g; Carbohydrates 28.4 g; Sugar 17.4 g; Protein 2.7 g; Cholesterol 0 mg

Refreshing Alkaline Smoothie

Serves: 2 / Preparation time: 5 minutes / Cooking time: 5 minutes

½ cup ice cubes

1 tbsp ginger

¼ cup fresh mint leaves

½ cup parsley

1 cucumber, chopped

1 lemon juice

1 cup water

4 cups baby spinach

1 avocado

- Add all ingredients to the blender and blend until smooth and creamy.
- Serve immediately and enjoy.

Per Serving: Calories 267; Fat 20.6 g; Carbohydrates 20.6 g; Sugar 4 g; Protein 5.9 g; Cholesterol 0 mg

Almond Carrot Smoothie

Serves: 1 / Preparation time: 5 minutes / Cooking time: 5 minutes

3 carrots, shredded

1 tsp ground cinnamon

½ banana

1 scoop protein powder

1 tbsp almond butter

1 cup unsweetened almond milk

- Add all ingredients to the blender and blend until smooth and creamy.
- Serve immediately and enjoy.

Per Serving: Calories 391; Fat 14.6 g; Carbohydrates 42 g; Sugar 17.9 g; Protein 28.8 g; Cholesterol 65 mg

Blueberry Almond Smoothie

Serves: 1 / Preparation time: 5 minutes / Cooking time: 5 minutes

1 tbsp hemp seeds

½ cup blueberries

1 tsp ground cinnamon

½ banana

1 scoop protein powder

1 tbsp almond butter

1 cup unsweetened almond milk

- Add all ingredients to the blender and blend until smooth and creamy.
- Serve immediately and enjoy.

Per Serving: Calories 400; Fat 18.3 g; Carbohydrates 35 g; Sugar 16.1 g; Protein 30.3 g; Cholesterol 65 mg

Kiwi Cucumber Boosting Smoothie

Serves: 1 / Preparation time: 5 minutes / Cooking time: 5 minutes

1 cup spinach

1 cup ice cubes

1 kiwi fruit

½ banana

¼ cucumber

¼ cup coconut milk

- Add all ingredients to the blender and blend until smooth and creamy.
- Serve immediately and enjoy.

Per Serving: Calories 255; Fat 15.1 g; Carbohydrates 31.8 g; Sugar 17.4 g; Protein 4.2 g; Cholesterol 0 mg

Spinach Protein Smoothie

Serves: 2 / Preparation time: 5 minutes / Cooking time: 5 minutes

1½ cups unsweetened almond milk

½ cup yogurt

½ tsp cinnamon

1 tbsp protein powder

½ banana

2 cups spinach

- Add all ingredients to the blender and blend until smooth.
- Serve and enjoy.

Per Serving: Calories 396; Fat 21.2 g; Carbohydrates 36.2 g; Sugar 16.1 g; Protein 19.9 g; Cholesterol 7 mg;

Tropical Smoothie

Serves: 1 / Preparation time: 5 minutes / Cooking time: 5 minutes

¼ cup coconut water

½ cup yogurt

1 tbsp honey

2 tsp shredded coconut

½ cup mango

½ cup pineapple

1½ cups spinach

- Add all ingredients to the blender and blend until smooth and creamy.
- Serve immediately and enjoy.

Per Serving: Calories 275; Fat 3.3 g; Carbohydrates 53.5 g; Sugar 47.2 g; Protein 10 g; Cholesterol 7 mg

Berry Kale Smoothie

Serves: 1 / Preparation time: 5 minutes / Cooking time: 5 minutes

1 cup orange juice

½ cup yogurt

1 banana

¼ cup raspberries

½ cup strawberries

1 cup kale

- Add all ingredients to the blender and blend until smooth and creamy.
- Serve immediately and enjoy.

Per Serving: Calories 376; Fat 2.8 g; Carbohydrates 77.6 g; Sugar 48.7 g; Protein 12.8 g; Cholesterol 7 mg

Basil Kale Strawberry Smoothie

Serves: 1 / Preparation time: 5 minutes / Cooking time: 5 minutes

1 ½ cups unsweetened coconut milk

1 tbsp flax seeds

¼ cup basil

3 strawberries

½ banana

1 cup kale

- Add all ingredients to the blender and blend until smooth and creamy.
- Serve immediately and enjoy.

Per Serving: Calories 203; Fat 8.5 g; Carbohydrates 28.4 g; Sugar 9.1 g; Protein 4.4 g; Cholesterol 0 mg

Chia Strawberry Smoothie

Serves: 2 / Preparation time: 5 minutes / Cooking time: 5 minutes

4 drops liquid stevia

½ lemon juice

½ small beetroot, chopped

1 cup strawberries

4 romaine lettuce leaves, chopped

2 celery stalks, chopped

2 tbsp chia seeds

1 cup coconut water

- Add all ingredients to the blender and blend until smooth and creamy.
- Serve immediately and enjoy.

Per Serving: Calories 98; Fat 3 g; Carbohydrates 15 g; Sugar 9.2 g; Protein 3.6 g; Cholesterol 0 mg

Strawberry Banana Smoothie

Serves: 2 / Preparation time: 5 minutes / Cooking time: 5 minutes

1 cup unsweetened almond milk ½ cup strawberries

1 banana

- Add all ingredients to the blender and blend until smooth and creamy.
- Serve immediately and enjoy.

Per Serving: Calories 84; Fat 2.1 g; Carbohydrates 17.3 g; Sugar 9 g; Protein 1.4 g; Cholesterol 0 mg

Spinach Berry Smoothie

Serves: 2 / Preparation time: 5 minutes / Cooking time: 5 minutes

2 tbsp almond butter

½ tsp ground cinnamon

1 tbsp coconut oil

1 banana

1 cup mixed berries

2 cups unsweetened coconut milk

2 cups fresh spinach

- Add all ingredients to the blender and blend until smooth and creamy.
- Serve immediately and enjoy.

Per Serving: Calories 302; Fat 20.4 g; Carbohydrates 28.5 g; Sugar 13.1 g; Protein 5.4 g; Cholesterol 0 mg

Graprefruit Spinach Smoothie

Serves: 2 / Preparation time: 5 minutes / Cooking time: 5 minutes

10 drops of liquid stevia

4 oz water

2 cups baby spinach

1 avocado

2 grapefruits, peeled and deseeded

- Add all ingredients to the blender and blend until smooth and creamy.
- Serve immediately and enjoy.

Per Serving: Calories 253; Fat 19.9 g; Carbohydrates 20.1 g; Sugar 9.6 g; Protein 3.6 g; Cholesterol 0 mg

Coconut Smoothie

Serves: 1 / Preparation time: 5 minutes / Cooking time: 5 minutes

1 banana

1 tbsp coconut oil

1 cup coconut water

4 oz fresh coconut meat

- Add all ingredients to the blender and blend until smooth and creamy.
- Serve immediately and enjoy.

Per Serving: Calories 669; Fat 52.4 g; Carbohydrates 53.1 g; Sugar 27.7 g; Protein 6.9 g; Cholesterol 0 mg

Pear Spinach Smoothie

Serves: 1 / Preparation time: 5 minutes / Cooking time: 5 minutes

¼ tsp vanilla extract

1 tsp ginger, grated

1 tsp maple syrup

1 ½ tbsp almond butter

½ cup yogurt

1 pear, chopped

1 cup baby spinach

1 cup unsweetened almond milk

- Add all ingredients to the blender and blend until smooth and creamy.
- Serve immediately and enjoy.

Per Serving: Calories 388; Fat 18.9 g; Carbohydrates 43.3 g; Sugar 27.5 g; Protein 14.6 g; Cholesterol 7 mg

Detox Avocado Smoothie

Serves: 2 / Preparation time: 5 minutes / Cooking time: 5 minutes

1 tbsp coconut butter

1 tbsp ginger

1 cup spinach

1 cucumber

1 avocado

1 cup coconut water

- Add all ingredients to the blender and blend until smooth.
- Serve and enjoy.

Per Serving: Calories 310; Fat 24.7 g; Carbohydrates 22.8 g; Sugar 6.8 g; Protein 4.9 g; Cholesterol 0 mg;

Almond Blueberry Smoothie

Serves: 1 / Preparation time: 5 minutes / Cooking time: 5 minutes

1 cup coconut milk

1 tbsp coconut oil

1 tbsp hemp seed powder

1 tbsp ground flaxseed

1 tbsp chia seeds

1 tbsp almond butter

½ cup blueberries

1 cup spinach

- Add all ingredients to the blender and blend until smooth and creamy.
- Serve immediately and enjoy.

Per Serving: Calories 502; Fat 42.9 g; Carbohydrates 21.5 g; Sugar 8.1 g; Protein 11.6 g; Cholesterol 0 mg

Avocado Blueberry Smoothie

Serves: 1 / Preparation time: 5 minutes / Cooking time: 5 minutes

1 tsp chia seeds

½ cup unsweetened coconut milk

1 avocado

½ cup blueberries

- Add all ingredients to the blender and blend until smooth and creamy.
- Serve immediately and enjoy.

Per Serving: Calories 389; Fat 34.6 g; Carbohydrates 20.7 g; Sugar 11.2 g; Protein 4.8 g; Cholesterol 0 mg

Vegan Blueberry Smoothie

Serves: 2 / Preparation time: 5 minutes / Cooking time: 5 minutes

2 cups blueberries

1 tbsp hemp seeds

1 tbsp chia seeds

1 tbsp flax meal

1/8 tsp orange zest, grated

1 cup fresh orange juice

1 cup unsweetened almond milk

- Add all ingredients to the blender and blend until smooth and creamy.
- Serve immediately and enjoy.

Per Serving: Calories 212; Fat 6.6 g; Carbohydrates 36.9 g; Sugar 24.8 g; Protein 5.2 g; Cholesterol 0 mg

Berry Peach Smoothie

Serves: 2 / Preparation time: 5 minutes / Cooking time: 5 minutes

1 cup coconut water

1 tbsp hemp seeds

1 tbsp agave

½ cup strawberries

½ cup blueberries

½ cup cherries

½ cup peaches

- Add all ingredients to the blender and blend until smooth and creamy.
- Serve immediately and enjoy.

Per Serving: Calories 117; Fat 2.5 g; Carbohydrates 22.5 g; Sugar 16.4 g; Protein 3.5 g; Cholesterol 0 mg

Kiwi Green Smoothie

Serves: 2 / Preparation time: 5 minutes / Cooking time: 5 minutes

1 cup ice cubes

1 cup mango

2 dates, pitted and chopped

1 lime, peeled

1/8 tsp lemon zest, grated

½ avocado, peeled and pitted

4 ripe kiwis, peeled and quartered

2 cups baby spinach

1 cup coconut water

- Add all ingredients to the blender and blend until smooth and creamy.
- Serve immediately and enjoy.

Per Serving: Calories 308; Fat 11.4 g; Carbohydrates 54.3 g; Sugar 34.3 g; Protein 5.5 g; Cholesterol 0 mg

Lemon Pineapple Smoothie

Serves: 2 / Preparation time: 5 minutes / Cooking time: 5 minutes

1 cup almond milk

1 tsp turmeric

½ lemon, peeled

2 cups pineapple

- Add all ingredients to the blender and blend until smooth and creamy.
- Serve immediately and enjoy.

Per Serving: Calories 362; Fat 29 g; Carbohydrates 30.4 g; Sugar 20.7 g; Protein 3.9 g; Cholesterol 0 mg

Raspberry Chia Smoothie

Serves: 2 / Preparation time: 5 minutes / Cooking time: 5 minutes

1 tsp vanilla extract

1 tbsp chia seeds

3 cups raspberries

1 cup coconut water

1 cup coconut milk

2 cups spinach

- Add all ingredients to the blender and blend until smooth and creamy.
- Serve immediately and enjoy.

Per Serving: Calories 425; Fat 31.3 g; Carbohydrates 35.2 g; Sugar 15.7 g; Protein 7.5 g; Cholesterol 0 mg

Orange Mango Avocado Smoothie

Serves: 2 / Preparation time: 5 minutes / Cooking time: 5 minutes

2 cups mango

½ tsp lime zest, grated

¼ cup avocado

½ cup water

1 ½ cups orange juice

- Add all ingredients to the blender and blend until smooth and creamy.
- Serve immediately and enjoy.

Per Serving: Calories 220; Fat 4.6 g; Carbohydrates 45.7 g; Sugar 38.3 g; Protein 3 g; Cholesterol 0 mg

Green Detox Smoothie

Serves: 2 / Preparation time: 5 minutes / Cooking time: 5 minutes

1 cup coconut water

½ lemon, peeled and chopped

½ cup pineapple chunks

1 cup mango chunks

1 carrot, chopped

½ tsp chia seeds

¼ tsp turmeric

¼ tsp ground cinnamon

½ tbsp ground ginger

½ celery stalk, chopped

1 apple, peeled, cored and chopped

¼ cup kale

2 cups baby spinach

- Add all ingredients to the blender and blend until smooth and creamy.
- Serve immediately and enjoy.

Per Serving: Calories 206; Fat 1 g; Carbohydrates 49.2 g; Sugar 34.9 g; Protein 3.9 g; Cholesterol 0 mg

Apricot Spinach Smoothie

Serves: 1 / Preparation time: 5 minutes / Cooking time: 5 minutes

½ tbsp coconut oil

1 cup coconut water

1 apricot

2 cups spinach

- Add all ingredients to the blender and blend until smooth.
- Serve and enjoy.

Per Serving: Calories 135; Fat 7.7 g; Carbohydrates 14.9 g; Sugar 9.7 g; Protein 3.9 g; Cholesterol 0 mg;

Healthy Melon Smoothie

Serves: 3 / Preparation time: 5 minutes / Cooking time: 5 minutes

1 cup ice cubes

1/8 tsp sea salt

1 tbsp flax meal

1 tbsp ginger

½ avocado, peeled and pitted

1 medium tangerine, peeled and segmented

1 cup arugula

2 cups honeydew melon, peeled and diced

2 cups cantaloupe, peeled and diced

1 cup orange juice

- Add all ingredients to the blender and blend until smooth and creamy.
- Serve immediately and enjoy.

Per Serving: Calories 215; Fat 8.1 g; Carbohydrates 36.2 g; Sugar 27.6 g; Protein 3.8 g; Cholesterol 0 mg

Cantaloupe Lemon Smoothie

Serves: 1 / Preparation time: 5 minutes / Cooking time: 5 minutes

1 tbsp fresh mint, chopped

10 drops liquid stevia

¼ cup coconut milk

1 tsp fresh lemon juice

1 cup cantaloupe, cubed

- Add all ingredients to the blender and blend until smooth and creamy.
- Serve immediately and enjoy.

Per Serving: Calories 195; Fat 14.7 g; Carbohydrates 16.6 g; Sugar 14.4 g; Protein 2.9 g; Cholesterol 0 mg

Frosty Watermelon Smoothie

Serves: 1 / Preparation time: 5 minutes / Cooking time: 5 minutes

1 tsp maple syrup

2 tbsp fresh lime juice

½ banana

2 cups watermelon, cut into chunks

¾ cup coconut water

- Add all ingredients to the blender and blend until smooth and creamy.
- Serve immediately and enjoy.

Per Serving: Calories 217; Fat 1 g; Carbohydrates 54.9 g; Sugar 36 g; Protein 4.1 g; Cholesterol 0 mg

Apple Beet Smoothie

Serves: 2 / Preparation time: 5 minutes / Cooking time: 5 minutes

6 dates

1 cup spinach

¼ tsp fresh ginger

1 small beet

1 apple, cored and sliced

2 cups coconut water

- Add all ingredients to the blender and blend until smooth and creamy.
- Serve immediately and enjoy.

Per Serving: Calories 200; Fat 0.9 g; Carbohydrates 48.7 g; Sugar 37.7 g; Protein 3.9 g; Cholesterol 0 mg

Matcha Green Smoothie

Serves: 1 / Preparation time: 5 minutes / Cooking time: 5 minutes

½ cup ice cubes

1/3 cup coconut milk

1/3 cup coconut water

¾ tsp matcha powder

1 cup spinach

¼ cup mint leaves

2 tbsp avocados

½ cup cucumber, chopped

- Add all ingredients to the blender and blend until smooth and creamy.
- Serve immediately and enjoy.

Per Serving: Calories 276; Fat 4.6 g; Carbohydrates 17.6 g; Sugar 6.6 g; Protein 4.7 g; Cholesterol 0 mg

Alkaline Super Smoothie

Serves: 1 / Preparation time: 5 minutes / Cooking time: 5 minutes

½ tsp maca root powder

1 cup coconut water

2 dates, pitted

1 tsp goji berries

5 oz raspberries

1 banana, peeled

- Add all ingredients to the blender and blend until smooth and creamy.
- Serve immediately and enjoy.

Per Serving: Calories 281; Fat 1.9 g; Carbohydrates 67.2 g; Sugar 38 g; Protein 5.6 g; Cholesterol 0 mg

Tomato Avocado Smoothie

Serves: 3 / Preparation time: 5 minutes / Cooking time: 5 minutes

¼ cup vegetable stock

½ tsp red pepper flakes

1 lime juice

1 cup spinach

3 tomatoes, chopped

2 avocados, peeled and chopped

1 ½ cucumber, chopped

- Add all ingredients to the blender and blend until smooth and creamy.
- Serve immediately and enjoy.

Per Serving: Calories 326; Fat 26.8 g; Carbohydrates 23.7 g; Sugar 6.9 g; Protein 5 g; Cholesterol 0 mg

Spinach Peach Banana Smoothie

Serves: 3 / Preparation time: 5 minutes / Cooking time: 5 minutes

1 cup baby spinach

2 cups coconut water

1 tbsp agave syrup

2 ripe bananas

2 ripe peaches, pitted and chopped

- Add all ingredients to the blender and blend until smooth and creamy.
- Serve immediately and enjoy.

Per Serving: Calories 163; Fat 0.9 g; Carbohydrates 39.2 g; Sugar 23.2 g; Protein 3.2 g; Cholesterol 0 mg

Salty Green Smoothie

Serves: 2 / Preparation time: 5 minutes / Cooking time: 5 minutes

1 cup ice cubes

¼ tsp liquid aminos

1 ½ tsp sea salt

1 garlic clove

2 limes, peeled and quartered

1 avocado, pitted and peeled

1 cup kale leaves

1 cucumber, chopped

2 cups tomato, chopped

¼ cup water

- Add all ingredients to the blender and blend until smooth and creamy.
- Serve immediately and enjoy.

Per Serving: Calories 299; Fat 20.3 g; Carbohydrates 32.2 g; Sugar 8.9 g; Protein 6.1 g; Cholesterol 0 mg

The "Dirty Dozen" And "Clean 15"

The Environmental Working Group (EWG) publishes annual lists of produce containing the highest and lowest levels of pesticide residue. The lists are based on analyzing data from the USDA Pesticide Data Program report.

The EWG found that a majority (70%) of the 48 different kinds of produce tested contained some residue of at least one type of pesticide. Overall they found 178 different kinds of pesticides. This pesticide residue can remain on produce despite washing and peeling. Every kind of pesticide is toxic for people and ingesting them can cause damage to the immune system, reproductive system, nervous system, cancer, and more. Pregnant women may harm the health and development of the unborn baby as a result of consuming pesticide residue.

Keep these facts in mind when you are selecting produce and deciding whether to buy organic.

The Dirty Dozen
- Celery
- Pears
- Spinach
- Strawberries
- Apples
- Nectarines
- Peaches
- Grapes
- Cherries
- Sweet bell peppers
- Tomatoes
- Potatoes

The Clean 15
- Eggplant
- Cauliflower
- Sweet corn
- Pineapples
- Avocados
- Onions
- Cabbage
- Frozen sweet peas
- Asparagus
- Papayas
- Mangoes
- Honeydew
- Cantaloupe
- Kiwi
- Grapefruit

Measurement Conversion Tables

Volume Equivalents (Dry)

US Standard	Metric (Approx.)
¼ teaspoon	1 ml
½ teaspoon	2 ml
1 teaspoon	5 ml
1 tablespoon	15 ml
¼ cup	59 ml
½ cup	118 ml
1 cup	235 ml

Weight Equivalents

US Standard	Metric (Approx.)
½ ounce	15 g
1 ounce	30 g
2 ounces	60 g
4 ounces	115 g
8 ounces	225 g
12 ounces	340 g
16 oz or 1 lb	455 g

Volume Equivalents (Liquid)

US Standard	US Standard (ounces)	Metric (Approx.)
2 tablespoons	1 fl oz	30 ml
¼ cup	2 fl oz	60 ml
½ cup	4 fl oz	120 ml
1 cup	8 fl oz	240 ml
1 ½ cups	12 fl oz	355 ml
2 cups or 1 pint	16 fl oz	475 ml
4 cups or 1 quart	32 fl oz	1 L
1 gallon	128 fl oz	4 L

Oven Temperatures

Fahrenheit (F)	Celsius (C) (Approx)
250°F	120°C
300°F	150°C
325°F	165°C
350°F	180°C
375°F	190°C
400°F	200°C
425°F	220°C
450°F	230°C

Alphabetical Recipe Index

Alkaline Super Smoothie	73
Almond Blueberry Smoothie	58
Almond Carrot Smoothie	44
Apple Beet Smoothie	71
Apple Spinach Cucumber Smoothie	31
Apricot Spinach Smoothie	67
Avocado Blueberry Smoothie	59
Avocado Mango Smoothie	37
Banana Peach Smoothie	42
Basil Kale Strawberry Smoothie	50
Berry Kale Smoothie	49
Berry Peach Smoothie	61
Blueberry Almond Smoothie	45
Broccoli Green Smoothie	33
Cantaloupe Lemon Smoothie	69
Chia Strawberry Smoothie	51
Coconut Smoothie	55
Detox Avocado Smoothie	57
Frosty Watermelon Smoothie	70
Graprefruit Spinach Smoothie	54
Green Detox Smoothie	66
Healthy Green Smoothie	30
Healthy Melon Smoothie	68
Healthy Vegetable Smoothie	34
Kiwi Cucumber Boosting Smoothie	46
Kiwi Green Smoothie	62
Lemon Pineapple Smoothie	63
Matcha Green Smoothie	72
Mix Berry Watermelon Smoothie	29
Orange Mango Avocado Smoothie	65
Pear Kale Smoothie	41
Pear Spinach Smoothie	56
Raspberry Chia Smoothie	64

Refreshing Alkaline Smoothie	43
Refreshing Green Smoothie	35
Refreshing Lime Smoothie	32
Salty Green Smoothie	76
Spinach Berry Smoothie	53
Spinach Coconut Almond Smoothie	40
Spinach Kale Green Smoothie	39
Spinach Peach Banana Smoothie	75
Spinach Protein Smoothie	47
Strawberry Banana Smoothie	52
Super Healthy Green Smoothie	38
Sweet Green Smoothie	36
Tomato Avocado Smoothie	74
Tropical Smoothie	48
Vegan Blueberry Smoothie	60
Watermelon Kale Smoothie	28
Watermelon Strawberry Smoothie	27

Made in the USA
Middletown, DE
18 April 2019